COOKING WITH COCONUT OIL

50 HEALTH CONSCIOUS

RECIPES WITH THE USE OF COCONUT OIL

Stir Fry, Pan Fry, Oven Baked, Soups, Salads, Sauces, & Many More...

Volume 2

Samantha Sterling

Copyright Recipe Junkies

All Rights Reserved

Table of Contents

Coconut Oil Healthy Chicken Stir Fry 6

Fried Chicken – Southern Recipe 8

Toasted Coconut Stuffed Avocado 10

Shrimp and Carrot Coconut-Ginger Quinoa 12

Tasty Coconut Chicken 14

Coconut Shrimp Curry 16

Spicy Garlic Shrimp Over Coconut Rice 18

Coconut Chicken Fingers 20

Sweet Chili Mayo Over Coconut Shrimp 22

Broccoli and Peanut Stir Fry 24

Pesto Thai Shrimp 26

Pan Grilled Burritos 28

Edamame and Sweet Potato Coconut Hash 30

Sage, Pecan, and Coconut Pork Tenderloin Cutlets 32

Mango-Coconut Chicken Wraps 34

Thai Halibut with Coconut-Curry Broth 36

Thai Chicken-Coconut Chicken Soup 38

Ceylonese Coconut Cashew Chicken 41

Coconut, Ginger, and Currant Rice 44

Raw Vegetable-Coconut Nori Rolls with Sunflower Seed Dipping Sauce 46

Paleo Jerk Chicken with Coconut, Mango, Pineapple Salsa 48

Spicy Beef & Cucumber Salad with Cashew-Coconut Rita 50

Thai-Mex-Coconut Snapper 53

Spicy Tom-Yum Coconut Noodles 55

Ceylon Coconut Pork Curry 57

Little Coconut Thai Turkey Loaves 59

Curried Coconut Chicken Lettuce Wraps 62

Thai Peanut, Coconut, and Panko Crusted Pork Chops 64

Spicy Sesame, Coconut, Honey Chicken Slow Cooked 66

Coconut Shrimp Mini Slider with Tropical Sauce 68

Coconut Chicken Soup 70

6 Ingredient Coconut Curry 72

Sticky Coconut Rice with Mango 74

Honey Coconut Salmon 76

Sweet and Sour Coconut Pork Sliders 78

Sweet and Sour Coconut Eggplant 81

Pork Souvlaki with Honeyed Coconut Apricots 83

Coconut Porchetts 85

Hawaiian Bacon 87

Simple Coconut Brined Turkey 89

Maple Apple and Coconut Pork Medallions 91

Bourbon, Coconut, Peach BBQ Pork Chops 93

Coconut Butter Beef Brisket 95

Hawaiian Harvest Pork Chops 96

Cheesy Sausage Hawaiian Pizza 98

Coconut Marinated Grilled Shrimp 100

Garlic and Coconut Prime Rib 102

Firecracker Coconut Grilled Alaska Salmon 104

Pork Chops with Raspberry Coconut Sauce 106

Pineapple Coconut Chicken Tenders 108

Coconut Oil Healthy Chicken Stir Fry

Ingredients:

- 1 Tbsp. of Coconut Oil
- ½ Cup of Fresh Sliced Carrots
- 2 tsp. of Minced Garlic
- 2 tsp. of Minced Ginger
- 1 Cup of Chicken – Cooked
- 2 tsp. of Hoisin Sauce
- 2 Tbsp. of Low Sodium Soy Sauce
- 1 Cup of Freshly Sliced Mushrooms
- 1 Bushel of Scallions – Chopped
- ½ Cup of Broccoli – Chopped

Directions:

1. Heat the coconut oil in a large frying pan with high heat.

2. Add in the carrots, ginger, and garlic.

3. Cook the carrots until the mixture is tender.

4. Stir in the chicken, soy sauce, and hoisin sauce.

5. Stir the mixture for 3-4 minutes.

6. Add in the scallions, mushrooms, and the broccoli.

7. Cook the mixture for another 2 minutes and serve the dish.

Nutritional Information:

- Calories: 235
- Total Fat: 3g
- Saturated Fat: 1g
- Carbohydrates: 2g
- Protein: 30g

Fried Chicken – Southern Recipe

Ingredients:

- 5 Pounds of Chicken Leg – Quarters
- 1 tsp. of Salt
- 1 tsp. of Pepper
- 1 tsp. of Garlic Powder
- 1 tsp. of Paprika
- 1 Cup of Coconut Flour
- Vegetable Oil

Directions:

1. In a large mixing bowl, add in the salt, pepper, paprika, garlic powder, and the chicken.

2. Use your hands to massage the seasonings into the meat. Make sure it is coated well.

3. Cover the chicken and sit it in the refrigerator for at least 2 hours; overnight is better.

4. Add your coconut flour to the chicken and toss it in order to coat it very well.

5. Heat the oil in a large frying pan to 375 degrees Fahrenheit; should be at least 2 inches in depth. (Cast iron pans work best.)

6. Add the chicken to the pan in batches. Make sure not to over crowd the chicken or it will not crisp.

7. Cook the chicken for 8 minutes on both sides until it is golden brown.

8. Using a thermometer, make sure the inside of the chicken is at least 165 degrees Fahrenheit.

Nutritional Information:

- Calories: 425
- Total Fat: 32g
- Saturated Fat: 7g
- Carbohydrates: 1g
- Protein: 34g

Toasted Coconut Stuffed Avocado

Ingredients:

- **2 Ripened Avocado (Sliced and pitted.)**
- **1 ½ Cups of Edamame – Shelled**
- **½ Cup of Unsweetened Coconut – Toasted**
- **2 Tbsp. of Diced Red Onion**
- **2 Tbsp. of Parsley – Chopped**
- **2 Tbsp. of Nori – Chopped**
- **1 tsp. of Dijon Mustard**
- **1 tsp. of Sesame Oil**
- **1 tsp. of Soy Sauce**
- **3 Tbsp. of Lemon Juice**
- **2 Tbsp. of Olive Oil**
- **Dash of Pepper**
- **Dash of Salt**

Directions:

1. In a large mixing bowl, add in the edamame, coconut, red onion, parsley, sesame seeds, and nori.

2. In a small mixing bowl, add in the sesame oil, mustard, soy sauce, and the lemon juice.

3. Whisk the olive oil into the mustard mixture slowly. Add in the salt and pepper to taste.
4. Pour the filling into the avocado.

Nutritional Information:

- Calories: 260
- Total Fat: 29g
- Saturated Fat: 7g
- Carbohydrates: 18g
- Protein: 8g

Shrimp and Carrot Coconut-Ginger Quinoa

Ingredients:

- Olive Oil
- 1 Cup of Quinoa
- 2 Cups of Chicken Stock
- 3 Tbsp. of Coconut Flakes
- ½ Cup of Grated Carrots
- ¼ Cup of Diced Onion
- 1 tsp. of Ginger – Grated
- ½ tsp. of Minced Garlic
- 10 Deveined Shrimp
- Lime Juice
- Cilantro – Garnish

Directions:

1. Cook the stock and the quinoa using the directions on the package.
2. Toast the coconut flakes in a medium sized pan and set it aside.
3. Coat a large pan with olive oil and sauté the carrots and onions until they are tender.
4. Add the ginger and the garlic and cook for another minute. Set it aside.

5. In the same pan, sauté the shrimp until it is brown.
6. When the quinoa is cooked, toss the coconut flakes, onions, carrots, ginger, and garlic into it.
7. Add in the minced cilantro and the lime juice.
8. Top it with the shrimp.

Nutritional Information:

- Calories: 210
- Total Fat: 23g
- Saturated Fat: 7g
- Carbohydrates: 76g
- Protein: 20g

Tasty Coconut Chicken

Ingredients:

- 1 Cup of Flour – Divided
- 1 Egg
- 1 Cup of Coconut Flakes – Sweetened
- ½ tsp. of Garlic Powder
- ½ tsp. of Salt
- ¼ tsp. of Pepper
- 4 Pieces of Boneless Chicken Breast
- ¼ Cup of Melted Butter

Directions:

1. Preheat your oven to 400 degrees Fahrenheit.
2. Line a baking sheet with some parchment paper.
3. Place ½ cup of flour in a large mixing bowl and set it aside.
4. In another mixing bowl, beat the egg.
5. In another mixing bowl add in the remaining flour with the coconut, salt, pepper, and garlic powder.
6. Dip the chicken in the plain flour and coat it well.

7. Dip the chicken into the beaten egg then into the coconut mixture.
8. Place it on the lined baking sheet.
9. When all the chicken is coated, bake the chicken for 30-40 minutes. (Flip the chicken half way through.)

Nutritional Information:

- Calories: 510
- Total Fat: 30g
- Saturated Fat: 21g
- Carbohydrates: 29g
- Protein: 31g

Coconut Shrimp Curry

Ingredients:

- **2 Tbsp. of Butter**
- **1 ½ Pounds of Shrimp**
- **1 Medium Onion – Finely Diced**
- **4 Minced Cloves of Garlic**
- **1 Tbsp. of Powdered Curry**
- **1 Can of Coconut Milk**
- **2 Tbsp. of Honey**
- **¼ tsp. of Salt**
- **Lime Juice**
- **Hot Sauce**
- **12 Basil Leaves**
- **2 Cups of Basmati Rice – Cooked**

Directions:

1. In a large pan over medium heat, add the butter.
2. Cook the shrimp on each side for 3 minutes. (Cook until they are opaque.) Set them aside.
3. Add in the onion, garlic, and ginger into the pan.
4. Sprinkle the curry on the top.
5. Add in the coconut milk and stir the mixture.

6. Add the lime juice, hot sauce, and honey.
7. Cook it on medium heat until it bubbles.
8. Add the shrimp and the basil. Allow it to cook for another minute.
9. Put a spoonful of shrimp mixture over the rice.

Nutritional Information:

- Calories: 210
- Total Fat: 23g
- Saturated Fat: 16g
- Carbohydrates: 63g
- Protein: 29g

Spicy Garlic Shrimp Over Coconut Rice

Ingredients:

- 1 ½ Cups of Long Grain Rice
- 1 Pound of Jumbo Shrimp – Peeled, Deveined
- 6 Large Minced Garlic Cloves
- 1 ½ Cups of Water
- Dash of Salt
- 1 Jalapeno – De-Ribbed, De-Seeded
- 1 Lime
- 1 Tbsp. of Olive Oil
- 5 2/3 Ounces of Coconut Milk
- 1 Tsp. of Red Chili Powder
- Cilantro

Directions:

1. Cook the rice according to the package directions.
2. In a blender, chop the garlic with water and ½ teaspoon of salt. Make sure there is still bits of garlic; a few pulses should do.
3. Pour the mixture over the shrimp and let it sit for 10 minutes.

4. Strain the water away from the shrimp and the garlic.
5. Add in the lime juice, ½ teaspoon of salt, and jalapeno.
6. Heat one tablespoon of olive oil over high heat in a large pan.
7. Add in the shrimp and cook it for one minute.
8. Add one small can of coconut milk and cook it for another 30 seconds.
9. Mix the chili powder into the mixture.
10. Put the rice in a large bowl.
11. Mix in the 5.6-ounce can of the coconut milk into the rice.
12. Serve the shrimp over the rice and garnish it with cilantro.

Nutritional Information:

- Calories: 610
- Total Fat: 18g
- Saturated Fat: 10g
- Carbohydrates: 77g
- Protein: 34g

Coconut Chicken Fingers

Ingredients:

- 4 Boneless Chicken Breasts – Cut into ½ inch Strips
- ½ tsp. of Salt
- ¼ tsp. of Red Pepper
- 1 Cup of Rice Flour
- 1 Cup of Buttermilk
- 1 Large Egg
- 1 ½ Cups of Unsweetened Shredded and Dried Coconut
- 3 Tbsp. of Canola Oil
- Sweet Chili Sauce

Directions:

1. Sprinkle the chicken with the pepper and the salt.
2. Put the flour in a shallow dish.
3. In a medium-mixing bowl, add in the egg and the buttermilk. Mix it well.
4. Put the coconut in a shallow dish.
5. Dredge all chicken through the flour and shake off the excess.

6. Dip the chicken into the egg mixture and then dredge through the coconut.
7. Heat a large frying pan over medium heat.
8. Add the oil to the pan.
9. Add in the chicken. Allow it to cook for 6 minutes on each side.
10. Serve it with the chile sauce if desired.

Nutritional Information:

- Calories: 290
- Total Fat: 15g
- Saturated Fat: 7g
- Carbohydrates: 34g
- Protein: 5g

Sweet Chili Mayo Over Coconut Shrimp

Ingredients:

- 1 Cup of Mayonnaise
- 2 Tbsp. of Sweet Chili Sauce
- 1 tsp. of Hot Sauce
- 1 Pound of Shrimp – Shelled, keep tail
- ½ Cup of Flour
- 1 Egg
- 2 Tbsp. of Coconut Milk
- Dash of Salt
- Dash of Pepper
- ½ Cup of Panko Breadcrumbs
- ½ Cup of Sweetened Coconut Flakes
- Frying Oil

Directions:

1. In a small mixing bowl, add the sweet chili sauce, mayonnaise, and hot sauce.
2. Using a paring knife, cut down the deep of the middle part of the back of the shrimp; discard the black vein.
3. In three shallow bowls, put flour in one, whisk the egg in another, and put the coconut in the last one.

4. Combine the panko to the coconut flakes.
5. In a large frying pan, add in 2 inches of oil and heat it over medium heat until it is 350 degrees Fahrenheit.
6. While the oil heats, dip the shrimp in the flour and shake off the excess.
7. Dip the shrimp into the egg, then the coconut flakes.
8. Fry the shrimp in smaller batches for 3 minutes until it is golden brown on both sides.
9. Serve the shrimp with sweet chili mayo for shrimp dipping.

Nutritional Information:

- Calories: 410
- Total Fat: 22g
- Saturated Fat: 9g
- Carbohydrates: 26g
- Protein: 28g

Broccoli and Peanut Stir Fry

Ingredients:

- 1 – 16 Ounce Package of Tofu – Firm
- 2 Cups of Uncooked Rice – Brown
- ½ tsp. of Salt
- 1 ½ Cups of Vegetable Broth
- 1 Tbsp. of Brown Sugar – Light
- 2 Tbsp. of Lime Juice
- 2 Tbsp. of Chili Sauce – Sweet
- 2 Tbsp. of Peanut Butter – Creamy
- 1 Tbsp. of Soy Sauce – Lite
- 1 tsp. of Ginger
- ¾ tsp. of Cornstarch
- 1 Tbsp. of Vegetable or Peanut Oil
- 1 tsp. of Sesame Oil – Dark
- 2 Cups of Broccoli Florets
- 1 Cup of Carrot Sticks
- 2 Tbsp. of Peanuts – Chopped
- Lime Wedges for Garnish

Directions:

1. Put the tofu in between 2 flat plates.

2. Put a heavy can on top of the plates. (The tofu should come out of the sides. Let it stand for 45 minutes.)
3. Cut the tofu into half-inch cubes.
4. Cook the rice using the instructions on the package and add the salt.
5. In a medium-mixing bowl, add in the oil and tofu.
6. Add the vegetables and sauté them until they are browned; 10 minutes.
7. Add in the tofu and sauté for another 5 minutes.
8. Add the marinade and bring it to a boil or until it is thick.

Nutritional Information:

- Calories: 400
- Total Fat: 13g
- Saturated Fat: 2.1g
- Carbohydrates: 58g
- Protein: 15.3g

Pesto Thai Shrimp

Ingredients:

- 1 ½ Pounds of Unpeeled Raw Shrimp – Large

Coconut Lime Rice
- 3 Tbsp. of Lime Juice
- 2 Tbsp. of Dry Roasted Peanuts – Unsalted
- 2 Tbsp. of Ginger
- 2 Minced Cloves of Garlic
- 1 tsp. of Salt
- 2 tsp. of Honey
- ½ tsp. of Red Pepper – Crushed
- ¼ Cup of Olive Oil
- 1 ½ Cup of Coconut

Directions:

1. Peel and devein the shrimp.
2. Put the oil, lime juice, peanuts, ginger, coconut, garlic, salt, and honey into a food processor. (For 20 seconds.)
3. Sauté the shrimp with 1 Tbsp. of oil in a large frying pan. It will take 3-5 minutes.

4. Stir the cilantro mixture into the shrimp and serve over the rice.

Nutritional Information:

- Calories: 300
- Total Fat: 13.9g
- Saturated Fat: 3.7g
- Carbohydrates: 23.9g
- Protein: 21g

Pan Grilled Burritos

Ingredients:

- **2 Cups of Chopped Chicken Breast – Cooked**
- **1 – 15 Ounce Can of Black Beans – Rinsed**
- **1 – 11 Ounce Can of Yellow Corn with Red/Green Bell Peppers – Drained**
- **1 Cup of Shredded Cheddar Cheese – 2%**
- **8 – 8 Inch Whole Wheat Flour Tortillas – Warmed**
- **Vegetable Cooking Spray**
- **Salsa**

Directions:

1. Put the chicken, beans, yellow corn, and cheese in a large mixing bowl.
2. Add in the cheese and stir it well.
3. Spray a large frying pan with cooking spray.
4. Heat the pan with medium heat.
5. Wrap up some mixture in a flour tortilla and place in the pan.
6. Press down with the spatula for 3-4 minutes.
7. Serve with creamy cilantro sauce.

Nutritional Information:

- Calories: 342
- Total Fat: 10.3g
- Saturated Fat: 4.4g
- Carbohydrates: 37.2g
- Protein: 23.2g

Edamame and Sweet Potato Coconut Hash

Ingredients:

- 1 – 8 Ounce Package of Smoked Lean Ham – Diced
- 1 Finely Chopped Onion - Sweet Freakings 1 Tbsp. of Olive Oil
- 2 Sweet Potatoes – Peeled, Cut into ¼ Inch Cubes
- 1 Minced Garlic Clove
- 1 Cup of Shredded Coconut
- 1 – 12 Ounce Package of Frozen Shelled Edamame
- 1 – 12 Ounce Package of Frozen Whole Kernel Corn
- ¼ Cup of Chicken Broth
- 1 Tbsp. of Chopped Thyme
- ½ tsp. of Salt
- ½ tsp. of Pepper

Directions:

1. Sauté the ham and onion over medium heat for 6-8 minutes.
2. Stir in the sweet potatoes and sauté it for 5 minutes.

3. Add in the garlic and sauté for 1 minute.
4. Stir in the edamame, coconut, corn, broth, and thyme.
5. Reduce the heat to medium and cover the mixture.
6. Cook it for 10-12 minutes and stir occasionally.
7. Add the salt and pepper to taste.

Nutritional Information:

- Calories: 192
- Total Fat: 5.8g
- Saturated Fat: 0.8g
- Carbohydrates: 22.1g
- Protein: 13.9g

Sage, Pecan, and Coconut Pork Tenderloin Cutlets

Ingredients:

- 1 Cup of Red Wine Vinegar
- 5 Tbsp. of Blackberry Preserves – Seedless
- ½ tsp. of Salt
- ½ Cup of Coconut
- 1 Pound of Pork Tenderloin
- ¾ Cup of Breadcrumbs
- ½ Cup of Pecans – Finely Chopped
- 4 tsp. of Olive Oil
- 2 Eggs - Beaten
- Spinach Leaves – Fresh
- Blackberries – Fresh

Directions:

1. In a small saucepan, bring vinegar to a boil over medium high heat.
2. Reduce the heat to medium and cook it for 6 minutes.
3. Stir in the preserves and cook it for 5 minutes.

4. Stir in the salt.
5. Remove the silver skin from the tenderloin. Leave the thin layer of fat.
6. Cut the pork into eight slices.
7. Place the pork between sheets of plastic wrap.
8. Flatten it to ¼ inch thickness.
9. In a medium mixing bowl, stir in the breadcrumbs, sage, pecans, and coconut.
10. Beat the egg and put it into a shallow bowl.
11. Dredge the tenderloin through the breadcrumbs, then the egg, and once again in the breadcrumbs.
12. Cook the pork in 2 teaspoons of hot oil over medium heat. Cook it for 8 minutes. (Turn the meat every 2 minutes.)
13. Drizzle the vinegar over top and garnish.

Nutritional Information:

- Calories: 452
- Total Fat: 22.4g
- Saturated Fat: 3.9g
- Carbohydrates: 33.6g
- Protein: 29.6g

Mango-Coconut Chicken Wraps

Ingredients:

- **2/3 Cup of Vegetable Broth**
- **¼ Cup of Cilantro – Chopped**
- **1 Green Onion – Chopped**
- **1 Chopped Garlic Clove**
- **1 Tbsp. of Lime Juice**
- **1 Tbsp. of White Wine Vinegar**
- **½ tsp. of Sea Salt**
- **2 Mangoes – Peeled, Chopped, Divided**
- **½ tsp. of Serrano Chili Pepper – Seeded, Chopped**
- **1 ½ Pounds of Chicken Breast – Strips**
- **¼ tsp. of Salt**
- **Romaine Lettuce – Leaves**
- **10 – 8 Inch Flour Tortillas**
- **Wooden Picks**

Directions:

1. In a food processor, add in the broth, cilantro, coconut, onion, garlic, lime juice, vinegar, and salt. Process it until it is smooth.
2. Add 1 chopped mango, Chile pepper into the blend and process it until it is smooth.

3. Pour half of the mixture into a dish or plastic freezer bag. Add the chicken and let it set for one hour.
4. Take the chicken out and discard the marinade.
5. Sprinkle the salt onto the chicken. (1/4 tsp.)
6. Grill the chicken covered on medium high heat (350-400 degrees for 4 minutes on both sides.
7. Shred the chicken into small, bite sized pieces.
8. Stir the chicken, remaining mango, and cilantro mixture.
9. Put lettuce leaves on the tortillas and top it with the chicken.
10. Roll the tortillas up and keep them from unrolling with the picks.

Nutritional Information:

- Calories: 320
- Total Fat: 9g
- Saturated Fat: 3g
- Carbohydrates: 21g
- Protein: 15g

Thai Halibut with Coconut-Curry Broth

Ingredients:

- 2 tsp. of Vegetable Oil
- 4 Shallots – Finely Chopped
- 2 ½ tsp. of Red Curry Paste
- 2 Cups of Low Sodium Chicken Broth
- ½ Cup of Light Coconut Milk
- ½ tsp. of Salt
- Dash of Salt
- 4 – 6 Ounce Halibut Fillets – Remove Skin
- Spinach – Steamed
- ½ Cup of Chopped Cilantro
- 2 Scallions – Green Only – Sliced Thin
- 2 Tbsp. of Lime Juice
- Dash of Black Pepper
- 2 Cups of Brown Rice – Cooked

Directions:

1. Cook the rice per package instructions.
2. Steam 5 cups of fresh spinach leaves in the microwave for 2 minutes.
3. Using a large sauté pan, heat the olive oil on medium heat.

4. Add shallots and cook them until they are brown. Stir them occasionally.
5. Add the curry paste and continue cooking them until it is fragrant; 30 seconds.
6. Add in the chicken broth, ½ tsp. of slat, and coconut milk. Simmer it until it is reduced to 2 cups. This will take 5 minutes.
7. Season the halibut with a dash of salt.
8. Arrange the fish inside the pan.
9. Gently shake the sauté pan in order to coat the fish with the sauce.
10. Cover the halibut and cook it until the fish flakes easily using a fork. This will take 7 minutes.
11. Arrange a pile of spinach in the bottom of a soup plate.
12. Top the spinach with fish fillets.
13. Stir the scallions' cilantro, and lime juice into the sauce.
14. Ladle the sauce on top of the fish and serve it with rice.

Nutritional Information:

- Calories: 634
- Total Fat: 9g
- Saturated Fat: 8g
- Carbohydrates: 10g
- Protein: 21g

Thai Chicken-Coconut Chicken Soup

Ingredients:

- 4 Cups of Chicken Stock
- 3 Kaffir Lime Leaves
- 2 Thai Chiles – Small, Halved Lengthwise
- 2 Cloves of Garlic – Crushed
- 1 – 3 Inch piece of Ginger – Fresh, Peeled, Cut 4 Chunks
- 1 Stalk of Lemongrass – White Part Only, Cracked with Knife
- 1 ½ Cups of Chicken – Cooked, Shredded
- 1 – 13 Ounce Can Coconut Milk – Unsweetened
- 1 – 8 Ounce Can of Straw Mushrooms – Rinsed
- 2 Tbsp. of Thai Fish Sauce – Nam Pla
- 1 ½ tsp. of Sugar
- Juice from 4 Limes
- Dash of Salt
- Dash of Pepper
- ¼ Cup of Fresh Cilantro – Chopped

Directions:

1. Bring the chicken stock to a boil on medium heat using a soup pot.
2. Add the lime leaves, garlic, chiles, ginger, and the lemongrass.
3. Turn the heat to medium-low heat.
4. Cover the pot and allow it to simmer for 10 minutes.
5. Stir in the chicken, mushrooms, coconut milk, sugar, lime juice, and fish sauce.
6. Simmer for 5 minutes.
7. Sprinkle it with pepper and salt.
8. Ladle the soup in a soup bowl.
9. Garnish it with the cilantro.
10. Place the vegetables and chi8cken in a big stockpot on medium heat.
11. Pour in 3 quarts of cold water into the pot.
12. Add the thyme, peppercorns, and bay leaves. Allow it to come to a boil on medium-low heat.
13. As it cooks take out the pieces that rise to the surface; add water as necessary.
14. Take the chicken out and place it on a cutting board until it is cool enough to touch. Take off the skin and remove the bones. Shred the chicken.
15. Strain the stock through a sieve (fine) and put it into another pot.
16. Add the vegetables to the stock.

Nutritional Information:

- Calories: 455
- Total Fat: 9g
- Saturated Fat: 5g
- Carbohydrates: 10g
- Protein: 16g

Ceylonese Coconut Cashew Chicken

Ingredients:

- ½ tsp. of Ground Cumin
- ½ tsp. of Ground Coriander
- ½ tsp. of Ground Fenugreek
- ½ tsp. of Ground Fennel
- ¼ tsp. of Ground Cardamom
- ½ tsp. of Chili Powder
- 3 Tbsp. of Vegetable Oil
- 1 Shallot – Small, Finely Minced
- 2 Crushed Garlic Cloves
- 3 Ounces of Raw Cashews
- 1 Tbsp. of Unsweetened Dried Coconut
- 1 tsp. of Grated Ginger
- 1 Tbsp. of Tomato Paste – Double Concentrate
- Dash of Salt
- 2 Cups of Coconut Milk – Divided
- 1 Pounds of Chicken Thighs – Boneless, Skinless

Directions:

1. In a small mixing bowl, add the coriander, cumin, fenugreek, cloves, fennel, cinnamon, and cardamom.
2. Using a small sauté pan on medium-high heat.
3. Add 1 Tbsp. of oil and shallots. Sauté them until they are yellow and soft.
4. Add in the spice and garlic; sauté for another 2 minutes.
5. Using a food processor, turn the cashews into powder.
6. Add the spice mixture, ginger, coconut, chili, dash of salt, tomato paste, 3 Tbsp. of coconut milk, and 4 Tbsp. of water. Turn it into a fine paste.
7. Thoroughly coat all of the chicken with the paste and let it stand in the refrigerator for 4 hours.
8. Using a large sauté pan on medium heat, add the oil and allow it to heat up.
9. Placed the chicken into the pan and brown it gently for 4 minutes on each side.
10. Discard the excess oil and reduce the heat to a medium-low heat.
11. Pour the coconut milk into the sauté pan, deglaze, and allow the coconut milk to come to a boil.
12. Allow it to simmer (uncovered) for 20 minutes or until the sauce is thick.
13. Serve it with steamed rice, roti, or dosa.

Nutritional Information:

- Calories: 760
- Total Fat: 66g
- Saturated Fat: 32g
- Carbohydrates: 21g
- Protein: 27g

Coconut, Ginger, and Currant Rice

Ingredients:

- 1 Tbsp. of Vegetable Oil
- ½ Onion – Small, Finely Chopped
- 1 Clove of Garlic – Finely Chopped
- 1 Tbsp. of Grated Ginger
- 1 Cup of Rice
- 1 Cup of Light Coconut Milk
- 1 ½ Tbsp. of Chicken Bouillon
- 1 ½ Cups of Water
- 1 Cup of Raisins

Directions:

1. Heat the oil in a 12-inch skillet on medium-high heat.
2. Cook the onion, ginger, garlic, and rice until the rice is brown.
3. Stir in the coconut milk and bouillon.
4. Bring it to a boil on high heat.
5. Reduce the heat to medium and cook it for 5 minutes; stir it frequently.
6. Add the water and bring it to a boil again.
7. Reduce the heat to low and allow it to simmer for 10 minutes.

8. Stir in the raisins and allow it to boil using high heat.
9. Reduce the heat to low and allow it to simmer (covered) for another 5 minutes.

Nutritional Information:

- Calories: 210
- Total Fat: 3g
- Saturated Fat: 0g
- Carbohydrates: 47g
- Protein: 4g

Raw Vegetable-Coconut Nori Rolls with Sunflower Seed Dipping Sauce

Ingredients:

- 2 Tbsp. of Flour
- 4 tsp. of Curry Powder
- ¼ tsp. of Red Pepper
- 2 ½ Pounds of Boneless Beef Chuck Steak – Cut into 1 inch chunks.
- 1 ½ Cups of Baby Carrots
- 1 Large Potato – Cut into 1-inch chunks.
- 1 – 15 Ounce Can of Coconut Milk
- 1 Envelope of Onion Soup Mix
- 1 Cup of Green Peas – Frozen

Directions:

1. In a large mixing bowl, add the curry powder, flour, and red pepper.
2. Add in the beef; toss the beef to coat it.
3. Brown the beef.
4. Inside a slow cooker, add in the beef and the remaining ingredients (except the peas).
5. Cover the cooker and cook it on low for 8-10 hours or on high for 4-6 hours.

6. Stir in the peas and allow it to stand for 5 minutes.

Nutritional Information:

- Calories: 245
- Total Fat: 6g
- Saturated Fat: 2.3g
- Carbohydrates: 20g
- Protein: 27g

Paleo Jerk Chicken with Coconut, Mango, Pineapple Salsa

Ingredients:

- 4 Chicken Breasts
- 2 tsp. of Minced Onion
- 2 tsp. of Thyme
- 2 tsp. of Black Pepper
- 2 tsp. of Allspice
- ½ tsp. of Salt
- ½ tsp. of Cinnamon
- ½ of Nutmeg
- ½ tsp. of Ground Chipotle
- 1 Tbsp. of Honey
- 1 Tbsp. of Lime Juice
- 1 Tbsp. of Orange Juice
- ¼ Cup of Coconut Aminos
- ¼ Cup of Olive Oil
- 2 Tbsp. of Apple Cider Vinegar
- 1 Gallon Sized Freezer Bag

Directions:

1. In a small mixing bowl, add all ingredients (except for chicken) and mix it together.
2. Place half of the marinade into the freezer bag.
3. Put the chicken in the bag; refrigerate it for 8-24 hours.
4. Store the extra marinade in a covered bowl in the refrigerator.
5. Set your grill to medium heat.
6. Grill the chicken on each side for 6-8 minutes. (Internal temperature should read 160 degrees Fahrenheit.)
7. Baste the chicken 1-2 times during the grilling.
8. Allow the chicken to set for 3 minutes; serve with the salsa.

Nutritional Information:

- Calories: 300
- Total Fat: 17g
- Saturated Fat: 3g
- Carbohydrates: 12g
- Protein: 25g

Spicy Beef & Cucumber Salad with Cashew-Coconut Rita

Ingredients:

- 2 Tbsp. of Coconut Oil
- ½ Brown Onion – Finely Diced
- ½ Long Red Chill – Finely Diced, De-Seeded
- 1 Pound of Veef Mince
- 3 Cloves of Garlic – Finely Diced
- 1 tsp. of Tomato Paste
- ¾ tsp. of Ground Coriander Seeds
- ¾ tsp. of Ground Cumin
- ½ tsp. of Paprika
- Dash of Pepper
- Dash of Cinnamon
- Dash of Ground Cloves
- ¾ tsp. of Sea Salt

Cucumber Salad

- 2 Cups of Cucumber – Diced
- 2 Tbsp. of Cilantro
- Dash of Pepper

- **Dash of Salt**
- **2 Tbsp. of Olive Oil**
- **1 Tbsp. of Lemon Juice**
- **10 Mint Leaves**
- **Fresh Cashews**

Coconut-Cashew Dressing

- **¾ Cup of Raw Cashews – Soaked in Warm Water (1 Hour)**
- **½ Coconut Flakes**
- **½ Clove of Garlic – Diced**
- **1 Tbsp. of Lemon Juice**
- **¾ tsp. olf Tahini Paste**
- **2 Tbsp. of Water**
- **Dash of Sea Salt**

Directions:

1. Heat the coconut oil in a large frying pan and cook the onion and chill for 5 minutes until they are brown and soft.
2. Bring it heat back to high and add the beef mince.
3. Separate it using a wooden spoon add the garlic and cook it for 2-3 minutes until the meat is brown and the liquid begins to evaporate.
4. Add the spices, pepper, salt, and tomato paste.
5. Cook it for another 5 minutes on high.

6. Combine all of the salad ingredients (except for the mint) and mix it; set aside.
7. Put all of the cashew raita into a food processor and process it until it is smooth.
8. Using a spatula, scrape down all of the sides and add in just a little water so it is not as thick.
9. Combine the beef with cucumber salad and serve it with dollops of dressing, chill, and add the mint to the top.

Nutritional Information:

- Calories: 750
- Total Fat: 59g
- Saturated Fat: 26g
- Carbohydrates: 21g
- Protein: 42g

Thai-Mex-Coconut Snapper

Ingredients:

- 1 ½ Pounds of Boneless Red Snapper Fillets
- 2 Tbsp. of Vegetable Oil – Divided
- 1 Pasilla Chili Pepper – Dried
- 1 Onion – Medium, Chopped
- 1 Red Bell Pepper – Chopped
- 3 Ounces of Chiitake Mushrooms – Sliced
- 1 ½ tsp. of Grated Ginger
- 2 tsp. of Garlic – Chopped
- 1 Chili De Arbol – Chopped
- ½ Cup of Coconut Milk
- ¼ Cup of Mayonnaise
- 2 tsp. of Chicken Bouillon
- ½ Cup of Water

Directions:

1. Remove the stem and the seeds from the chile. Toast it in a dry skillet on medium heat. (Press it down with a spatula.)
2. Pour ½ cup of boiling water on the chili. Cover it and allow it to soak 10 minutes.

3. Process the pasilla chile with the soaking liquid in a small food processor and set it aside.
4. Sprinkle the snapper with the bouillon. Heat 1 Tbsp. of oil in a 12 inch deep skillet on medium-high heat.
5. Cook the snapper with the flesh side down until it is golden. This will take 3 minutes.
6. Heat the remaining 1 Tbsp. of oil in the same skillet and cook the red pepper, onion, and mushrooms; stir it frequently.
7. Stir in the ginger, chile, and garlic; cook it for 30 seconds.
8. Stir in the pasilla chili puree and cook it; stir it occasionally, until it is thick. (2 Minutes)
9. Stir in the coconut milk and water. Bring it to a boil on high heat.
10. Reduce the heat to low and add in the snapper.
11. Simmer the snapper until it flakes; 5 minutes.
12. Gently whisk in the mayonnaise.

Nutritional Information:

- Calories: 270
- Total Fat: 17g
- Saturated Fat: 5g
- Carbohydrates: 5g
- Protein: 25g

Spicy Tom-Yum Coconut Noodles

Ingredients:

- 2 Cups of Chicken Stock
- 1 Stalk of Lemongrass – Thinly Sliced
- 1 Inch of Ginger Root – Thinly Sliced
- 1 Garlic Clove – Large, Minced
- 12 Ounces of Kelp Noodles – Rinsed, Drained
- 1 Strip of Seaweed – Wakame, Chopped 2 Inch Pieces
- 2 Cups of Shitake Mushroom – Thinly Sliced
- 2 Cups of Coconut Milk
- 1 Tbsp. of Miso Paste
- 1 Tbsp. of Honey
- 1 tsp. of Coconut Aminos
- 11 Limes – Juice
- 4 Cilantro – Chopped

Directions:

1. In a large cooking pot, add in the first 6 ingredients and bring them to a light steam.
2. Turn the heat off and cover it with a lid tightly and allows it to steep for at least 20 minutes.

3. Add the shitakes and the coconut milk.
4. Bring it back to a light steam.
5. Whisk the remaining ingredients, garnish it with the cilantro and a few slices and lime wedges.

Nutritional Information:

- Calories: 460
- Total Fat: 32g
- Saturated Fat: 26g
- Carbohydrates: 20g
- Protein: 26g

Ceylon Coconut Pork Curry

Ingredients:

- 4 Tbsp. of Oil
- 20 Curry Leaves
- ¼ tsp. of Fenugreek Seeds
- 2 Onion – Large, Sliced
- 5 Cloves of Garlic – Chopped
- 1 Tbsp. of Ginger – Chopped
- 4 Pounds of Pork
- 3 Tbsp. of Curry Powder
- 2 Chiles – Chopped
- 2 tsp. of Salt
- 2 Tbsp. of Vinegar
- 2 tsp. of Sugar
- 1 Cup of Hot Water
- 13 Ounces of Coconut Milk

Directions:

1. Add oil to a medium frying pan.
2. Add in curry leaves and the fenugreek seeds. Heat for 1-2 minutes.
3. Add the garlic, onions, and ginger. Fry it over medium heat until it is brown. (20 minutes)

4. Add the diced pork, chillies, curry powder, salt, sugar, and vinegar. Toss the pork to it is coated with the spice mixture.
5. Add the hot water and cover the pan with a lid. Simmer it for 1.5-2 hours.
6. Add in the coconut milk. Allow it to simmer for 10 minutes.
7. Serve it with steamed rice.

Nutritional Information:

- Calories: 910
- Total Fat: 55g
- Saturated Fat: 27g
- Carbohydrates: 18g
- Protein: 88g

Little Coconut Thai Turkey Loaves

Ingredients:

- ¼ Cup of Peanut Butter
- 2 Cloves of Garlic – Quartered
- 1 Tbsp. of Ginger – Chopped
- 1 Hot Pepper – Small, De-Seeded
- ¼ Cup of Peanut Oil
- 2 Tbsp. of Soy Sauce
- 2 Tbsp. of Splenda
- 2 Tbsp. of Sesame Oil
- ¼ Cup of Teas
- 6 Scallions – Medium, Trim, Include the White and Green
- 1/3 Cup of Cilantro
- 1 Stalk Lemongrass
- 2 Cloves of Garlic
- 1 Pound of Ground Turkey
- ½ Cup of Brown Rice
- ¼ Cup of Unsweetened Low Fat Coconut Milk
- 1 Egg – Slightly Beaten
- ¼ Cup of Bread Crumbs
- ½ Cup of Peanut Sauce
- 2 Tbsp. of Sesame Oil
- ½ Cup of Coconut Milk

- ¼ Cup of Peanut Sauce
- 1 Tbsp. of Sugar

Directions:

1. Preheat your oven to 400 degrees Fahrenheit.
2. Coat a 6 muffin pan with nonstick cooking spray.
3. Puree all of the Peanut Sauce ingredients together.
4. In a blender, pulse together the cilantro, scallions, lemongrass, and garlic.
5. Put the mixture is a large mixing bowl.
6. Add the turkey, ½ cup of each of the coconut milks, rice, and peanut sauce; along with sesame oil.
7. Mix the mixture with your hands.
8. Pack the turkey mixture into the muffin pan.
9. Bake the turkey until the center reads 170 degrees Fahrenheit. (30-35 minutes)
10. Whisk the coconut milk, sugar, and peanut sauce together.
11. Warm the sugar/coconut mixture slightly.
12. Drizzle on the loaves of turkey.

Nutritional Information:

- Calories: 470
- Total Fat: 33g
- Saturated Fat: 10g
- Carbohydrates: 25g
- Protein: 20g

Curried Coconut Chicken Lettuce Wraps

Ingredients:

- 2 Cups of Cooked Chicken Meat – Chopped, Shredded
- 3 Scallions – White and Green Parts
- 1/3 Cup of Coconut Flakes
- ¼ Cup of Cilantro – Chopped
- 1 Stalk of Celery – Finely Chopped
- 1 Roma Tomato – Seeded, Diced
- ½ Cup of Frozen Peas – Thawed
- ¼ Cup of Dried Currants
- ¼ Cup of Lite Coconut Milk
- 1 ½ tsp. of Cumin
- ½ tsp. of Garlic – Granulated
- 1 White Wine Vinegar
- Sea Salt
- Red Leaf Lettuce

Directions:

1. In a mixing bowl, combine the chicken, scallions, cilantro, celery, tomato, peas, and the currants.
2. Whisk the coconut milk, curry powder, cumin, garlic, vinegar, and sea salt.

3. Add the dressing to the salad and toss it to coat it evenly.
4. Serve the salad wrapped in lettuce leaves.

Nutritional Information:

- Calories: 60
- Total Fat: 4g
- Saturated Fat: 3g
- Carbohydrates: 7g
- Protein: 2g

Thai Peanut, Coconut, and Panko Crusted Pork Chops

Ingredients:

- 4 – 1 inch Thick Boneless Pork Chops
- ¾ Cup of Roasted Peanuts – Unsalted
- ½ Cup of Coconut Flakes
- ¾ Cup of Panko Crumbs
- 1 Egg – Large
- 1 Tbsp. of Milk
- Coconut Oil
- Lime Wedges

Stuffing

- 3 Garlic Cloves
- 1 Slice of Ginger – ¼ Inch Thick
- 2 Stalks of Lemongrass – Lower Part, Chopped
- ¾ Cup of Cilantro Leaves
- 1 tsp. of Coconut Oil
- 1 Tbsp. of Fish Sauce

Directions:

1. Preheat your oven to 375 degrees Fahrenheit.
2. Trim the fat off of the pork chops and slice them to form a pocket.
3. Place the peanuts into the food processor until it is turned to crumbs. Put it into a shallow dish.
4. Place the ginger, garlic, lemongrass, coconut oil, cilantro, and fish sauce into the processor and pulse it until it is a thick paste.
5. Fill the chops with the mixture and stick a toothpick through the pork chop.
6. Whisk the milk, coconut, and the egg together in a shallow bowl.
7. Dip the pork chops into the egg mixture and place them in the peanut panko mixture.
8. Put 1/3 inch of oil in a large frying pan. Heat it over medium-high heat.
9. Fry the pork chops until they are golden brown on both sides. (6 minutes on both sides)

Nutritional Information:

- Calories: 270
- Total Fat: 18g
- Saturated Fat: 5g
- Carbohydrates: 22g
- Protein: 11g

Spicy Sesame, Coconut, Honey Chicken Slow Cooked

Ingredients:

- 1 ½ Pounds of Chicken Breasts
- 2 Tbsp. of Honey
- 1 tsp. of Sesame Oil
- 1 ½ Tbsp. of Rice Vinegar
- ½ tsp. of Sriracha
- 3 Tbsp. of Coconut Aminos
- 2 Tbsp. of Tomato Paste
- 2 Tbsp. of Water
- 2 tsp. of Arrowroot Starch
- 1 Garlic Cloves
- ½ Cup of Yellow Onion – Minced
- 1 tsp. of Jalapeno Chilies – Minced
- Lime Wedges
- Sesame Seeds
- Scallions

Directions:

1. Add the sesame oil, honey, aminos, tomato paste, rice vinegar, and sriracha in a medium mixing bowl.
2. Mine the garlic.
3. Chop the onion finely.
4. De-seed the peppers and chop them finely.
5. Add the garlic, onion, and peppers to the bowl.
6. In a separate bowl, mix the water and starch together. Add it to the mixture.
7. Put the chicken in the crock-pot and pour the sauce on the top.
8. Cook it on high for 3 ½ hours or on low for 5-7 hours.

Nutritional Information:

- Calories: 280
- Total Fat: 8g
- Saturated Fat: 2g
- Carbohydrates:18g
- Protein: 37g

Coconut Shrimp Mini Slider with Tropical Sauce

Ingredients:

- 1 – 12 Ounce Package of Coconut Shrimp
- 1/3 Cup of Mayonnaise
- 5 Slices of Muenster Cheese – Cut in half and then fold it over.
- Green Leaf Lettuce – Tear into 10 pieces.
- 10 Party Sized Potato Rolls – Split

Directions:

1. Cook the coconut shrimp using the package directions. Remove the tails.
2. Combine 2 Tbsp. of mayonnaise with the dipping sauce included in the coconut shrimp package.
3. Evenly spread the rolls with the mixture.
4. Add a piece of lettuce to the rolls, then the shrimp and cheese.
5. Push a toothpick through the top and garnish with a cube of mango, pineapple, or papaya.

Nutritional Information:

- Calories: 200
- Total Fat: 10g
- Saturated Fat: 1g
- Carbohydrates: 35g
- Protein: 4g

Coconut Chicken Soup

Ingredients:

- 3 Cups of Chicken Stock
- 1 Thumb Sized Piece of Ginger – Sliced
- 1 Cup of Coconut Milk
- 1 Tbsp. of Fish Sauce
- 2 tsp. of Honey
- 6 Ounces of Chicken
- 1 Cup of Mushrooms – Drained, Rinsed
- 1 Carrot – Medium, Julienned
- 2 Tbsp. of Lime Juice
- ¼ Cup of Cilantro – Minced

Directions:

1. In a large pot, add the chicken stock and the ginger. Bring it to a boil and allow it to simmer for 5 minutes.
2. Stir in the coconut milk, agave, fish sauce, carrot, and mushrooms.
3. Add in the limejuice and cilantro before you serve it.

Nutritional Information:

- Calories: 290
- Total Fat: 18g
- Saturated Fat: 13g
- Carbohydrates: 19g
- Protein: 17g

6 Ingredient Coconut Curry

Ingredients:

- 1 Can of Coconut Milk
- 2 Tbsp. of Red Curry Paste
- 2 Heads of Broccoli
- 1 Can of Garbanzo – Rinsed, Drained
- ½ Tbsp. Of Corn Starch – Dissolve in 2 Tbsp. of Cold Water
- Minced Garlic

Directions:

1. Sauté the broccoli and garlic using 1 Tbsp. of oil.
2. After 3 minutes of sautéing, add the coconut milk and allow it to simmer 5-8 minutes.
3. Add in the curry paste into the pan.
4. Whisk it very well.
5. Add in the chickpeas.
6. Bring it to a slight boil and add in the cornstarch.
7. Boil it for 1 minute.
8. Reduce the heat and allow it to slightly cool. (The sauce will thicken as it cools.)

Nutritional Information:

- Calories: 730
- Total Fat: 30g
- Saturated Fat: 22g
- Carbohydrates: 95g
- Protein: 32g

Sticky Coconut Rice with Mango

Ingredients:

- 1 ½ Cups of Sticky Rice
- 1 Cup of Coconut Milk – Unsweetened
- ½ Cup of Turbinado Sugar
- ½ tsp. of Salt
- 2 Mangos – Sliced
- 8 Mint Leaves – Garnish

Directions:

1. Put the sticky rice in a medium bowl and cover it with cold water. Allow it to soak overnight.
2. Drain the rice, place the rice in a microwave safe medium sized bowl.
3. Cover it with four cups of cold water.
4. Cover the bowl with a plate, and then microwave it for 3 minutes and stir.
5. Continue to microwave the rice and stir it every 3 minutes until the rice is fluffy. (10-12 minutes)
6. Put the coconut milk into a medium saucepan.
7. Turn the heat to medium and cook it until the milk is heated; yet not boiling.

8. Add the sugar and the salt; stir it until it is dissolved.
9. Move the rice to a large mixing bowl.
10. Cover it with coconut milk and stir the rice until it begins to absorb the liquid. Let it stand for 1 hour.
11. Top the rice with pieces of the mango and garnish it with mint.

Nutritional Information:

- Calories: 520
- Total Fat: 15g
- Saturated Fat: 13g
- Carbohydrates: 92g
- Protein: 7g

Honey Coconut Salmon

Ingredients:

- 1 ½ Cups of Butter
- ¾ Cup of Honey
- ¼ Cup of Brown Sugar
- ¾ Cup of Flake Coconut
- 4 – 4 Ounce Salmon Fillets

Directions:

1. Melt the butter in a medium saucepan on medium heat.
2. Mix in the brown sugar, honey, and coconut.
3. Bring the mixture to a boil and then remove it from the heat. Allow it to cool slightly.
4. Put the mixture in a large mixing bowl.
5. Put the salmon in the bowl and turn it to thoroughly goat the salmon.
6. Cover the bowl and allow it to sit in the refrigerator for 30 minutes.
7. Preheat your oven to 375 degrees Fahrenheit.
8. Spread the marinade mix in a baking dish in order to coat the bottom.
9. Arrange the salmon onto the dish and pour some of the marinade on top/

10. Bake the fish for 25 minutes. Bat it occasionally.

Nutritional Information:

- Calories: 1040
- Total Fat: 77g
- Saturated Fat: 49g
- Carbohydrates: 69g
- Protein: 24g

Sweet and Sour Coconut Pork Sliders

Ingredients:

Slaw

- 1 ½ Cups of Green Cabbage – Finely Sliced
- 1 ½ Cups of Red cabbage – Finely Sliced
- 2 Tbsp. of Seasoned Rice Vinegar
- 1 tsp. of Sesame Oil
- ¼ tsp. of Salt
- ¼ tsp. of Black Pepper
- 4 Green Onions – Thinly Sliced

Pork

- ½ Cup of Orange Juice
- ½ Cup of Soy Sauce
- ¼ Cup of Brown Sugar
- 2 ½ Tbsp. of Seasoned Rice Vinegar
- 2 Tbsp. of Sesame Oil
- ½ tsp. of Black Pepper
- 2 Cloves of Garlic – Minced

- 1 – 1 Inch Piece of Ginger – Peeled, Minced
- Zest of 1 Orange – Large
- 1 – 1 ½ Pounds of Pork Tenderloin – Trimmed
- 2 tsp. of Arrowroot
- 10-12 Mini Hawaiian Sweet Rolls – Halved, Horizontally
- ½ Cup of Coconut Flakes

Directions:

1. For the slaw: Toss the red and green cabbage, oil, vinegar, pepper, salt, and green onions in a large mixing bowl. Mix it together and place it in the refrigerator while the pork is prepared.
2. For the pork: In a large mixing bowl, whisk the orange juice, brown sugar, soy sauce, vinegar, sesame oil, garlic, pepper, ginger, and the orange zest together.
3. Add the tenderloin and coat it thoroughly. Refrigerate it for 1 hour.
4. Preheat your oven to 425 degrees Fahrenheit.
5. Place the pork on a nonstick baking pan and roast it until the thermometer reads 145 degrees Fahrenheit (25-30 minutes).
6. Remove the pork from the oven and allow it to stand 5-10 minutes.

7. Pour the marinade into a saucepan and whisk in arrowroot. Bring it to a boil on medium-high heat.
8. Once the sauce is thickened, remove it from the heat.
9. Transfer the tenderloin to a cutting board and cut it ¼ - 1/3 inch thick.
10. Divide the pork on the rolls and top it with the sauce, coconut, and slaw.

Nutritional Information:

- Calories: 320
- Total Fat: 17g
- Saturated Fat: 6g
- Carbohydrates: 19g
- Protein: 31g

Sweet and Sour Coconut Eggplant

Ingredients

- 2 Cups of Virgin Olive Oil
- 2 Tbsp. of Virgin Olive Oil – Cooking
- 2 Medium Sized Eggplants – Sliced to ½ Inch
- 2 Medium Sized Red Onion – ½ Inch Dice
- 3 Ribs of Celery – Cut into ½ inch pieces.
- 1 Cup of White Wine Vinegar
- 3 Tbsp. Of Sugar
- 1/3 Cup of Coconut Flakes
- Dash of Salt
- Dash of Pepper

Directions:

1. In a large frying pan heat the oil until it is almost to a smoking.
2. Very carefully add the slices of eggplant; working in batches. Do not crowd the pan.
3. Cook the eggplant until it is gold on both sides. Place cooked pieces on a paper towel lined pan.
4. In a large frying pan add in 2 Tbsp. of oil until it was almost smoking.

5. Add the celery and onions; sauté them until they are browned.
6. Remove it from the heat, and then add the vinegar, coconut flakes, salt, pepper, and sugar.
7. Place the cooled off eggplant in a large mixing bowl. Cover it with the vinegar mix and allow it to stand for 1 hour.

Nutritional Information:

- Calories: 358
- Total Fat: 19g
- Saturated Fat: 17g
- Carbohydrates: 13g
- Protein: 5g

Pork Souvlaki with Honeyed Coconut Apricots

Ingredients:

Souvlaki

- 2 Shallots – Minced
- 2 Cloves of Garlic – Minced
- 2 Tbsp. of Oregano
- 1 Jalapeno Pepper – Seeded, Minced
- Juice from 1 Lemon
- ½ Cup of Olive Oil
- 2 Pounds of Pork Tenderloin – Cut 1 ½ - 2 Inches Thick

Apricots

- Juice from 3 Limes
- ¾ Cup of Dry Rose Wine or White Wine
- ¼ Cup of Honey
- 1 Shallot – Minced
- 12 Big Dried Apricots
- 1 Tbsp. of Chopped Mint
- 1 Tbsp. of Pine Nuts – Toasted
- Greek Yogurt

Directions:

1. Add the shallots, oregano, garlic, lemon juice, jalapeno, and olive oil inside a large freezer bag.
2. Add the pork into the bag and let it sit in the refrigerator for 3 hours.
3. Soak 12-16 wooden Skewers in water for 20 minutes.
4. Bring the wine, honey, lime juice, and shallot to a simmer in a medium saucepan on medium heat.
5. Add the apricots and cook them in the mixture until they are syrupy; 12 minutes.
6. Preheat your grill to medium heat.
7. Remove the pork from the bag and thread 2 pieces on the skewers.
8. Grill them until it is cooked completely; 3-5 minutes on each side.
9. Fold the pine nuts and mint into the mixture.
10. Serve it with a dollop of the yogurt and mixture.

Nutritional Information:

- Calories: 477
- Total Fat: 19g
- Saturated Fat: 3g
- Carbohydrates: 28g
- Protein: 44g

Coconut Porchetts

Ingredients:

- 8 Ounces of Panetta – Finely Chopped
- 10 Cloves of Garlic – Minced
- Zest from 3 Lemons
- Zest from 1 Orange
- ½ Cup of Parsley
- Leave off 4 Sprigs of Rosemary
- 2 Tbsp. of Red Pepper Flakes
- 2 Tbsp. of Capers – Rinsed, Chopped
- ½ Cup of Coconut Meat
- Salt
- 1 – 10-12 Pound Boneless Ham – Skin-On

Directions:

1. Preheat your oven to 350 degrees Fahrenheit.
2. Put the pancetta and coconut in a food processor and pulse it until it is paste.
3. Transfer it to a bowl and mix it by hand with the zests, garlic, parsley, red pepper, rosemary, capers, and 2 Tbsp. of salt until it is thoroughly blended.
4. Put the ham (flesh side up_ on a cutting board. Score the meat.

5. Rub the pancetta mixture in the meat.
6. Flip the ham over on the other side and score it.
7. Put the pork inside a roasting pan; put in the oven for 2 hours.
8. Turn the oven temperature up to 400 degrees Fahrenheit and roast it until the pork internal temperature is 170 degrees Fahrenheit. (1.5 hours).
9. Remove the ham from the oven and allow it to rest for 30 minutes.

Nutritional Information:

- Calories: 330
- Total Fat: 32g
- Saturated Fat: 3g
- Carbohydrates: 0g
- Protein: 11g

Hawaiian Bacon

Ingredients:

- 5 Pounds of Pork Belly – Skin on
- ¼ Cup of Salt
- 1/3 Cup of Coconut Oil
- 2 tsp. of Pink Curing Salt
- ¼ Cup of Dark Brown Sugar
- ¼ Cup of Honey
- 2 Tbsp. of Red Pepper Flakes
- 2 Tbsp. of Smoked Paprika
- 1 tsp. of Cumin Seed

Directions:

1. Rinse the pork belly and pat it dry.
2. Transfer it to a re-sealable two-gallon freezer bag.
3. In a large mixing bowl, add the salt, brown sugar, pink salt, honey, red pepper, cumin, coconut oil, paprika, and cumin. Mix it thoroughly.
4. Coat the pork belly thoroughly.
5. Allow the pork belly to sit in the mix inside the refrigerator for 7-10 days. Flip it once a day.

6. Remove the pork from the bag and rinse it well, and then pat it dry.
7. Refrigerate the pork again for 2 days.
8. Using the smoker according to the manufacturers instructions, use apple-wood chips and set the smoker to 200 degress Fahrenheit.
9. Smoke the pork for 3 hours or the internal temperature goes to 150 degrees Fahrenheit.
10. Slice the bacon and fry it in a large frying pan.

Nutritional Information:

- Calories: 46
- Total Fat: 4g
- Saturated Fat: 1g
- Carbohydrates: 1g
- Protein: 3g

Simple Coconut Brined Turkey

Ingredients:

- 1 – 20 Pound Turkey
- 1 Cup of Salt
- 1 Gallon of Water
- ½ Cup of Sugar
- 1 Cup of Coconut Butter – Melted
- 1 Cup of Herbs
- 1 Large Kettle

Directions:

1. Combine all ingredients in a large container.
2. Stir it until the sugar and salt is dissolved.
3. Rinse the turkey thoroughly.
4. Put the turkey in the brine and cover it with plastic wrap.
5. Turn the turkey many time to evenly brine.
6. Remove it from the brine and rinse it thoroughly.
7. Roast it in your oven for 20 minutes per pound on 325 degrees Fahrenheit.

Nutritional Information:

- Calories: 153
- Total Fat: 1g
- Saturated Fat: 0g
- Carbohydrates: 0g
- Protein: 34g

Maple Apple and Coconut Pork Medallions

Ingredients:

- 1 ½ Cups of Apple Cider
- 3 Tbsp. of Cornstarch
- ¼ Cup of Pure Maple Syrup
- ½ Cup of Coconut Butter
- 2 Tbsp. of Apple Cider Vinegar
- 2 tsp. of Ground Mustard
- ¼ tsp. of Pepper
- ½ tsp. Saigon Cinnamon
- ¼ tsp. of Allspice
- 1 – 1 ½ Pounds of Pork Tenderloin – Cut in Medallions
- 1 Tbsp. of Canola Oil
- 2-3 Apples – Cored, Sliced

Directions:

1. In a large mixing bowl, add the cornstarch and apple cider, maple syrup, mustard, coconut butter, vinegar, pepper, allspice, and cinnamon. Whisk it thoroughly.
2. In large frying pan on medium-high heat, add the oil.

3. Put the pork medallions into the pan and brown them until they are brown on both sides. (2 minutes)
4. Continue cooking it for 4-6 minutes until the internal temperature reaches 145 degrees Fahrenheit.
5. Add the maple mixture to the pan and bring it to a boil.
6. Add in the apple slices and stir it well. Cook them for 4-6 minutes covered.
7. Add the pork to the skillet and allow it to simmer for 1-2 minutes.

Nutritional Information:

- Calories: 477
- Total Fat: 19g
- Saturated Fat: 3g
- Carbohydrates: 28g
- Protein: 44g

Bourbon, Coconut, Peach BBQ Pork Chops

Ingredients:

- **3 Pounds of Boneless Pork Loin**
- **1 Tbsp. of Coconut Oil**
- **Salt**
- **Pepper**
- **4 Peaches**
- **6 Ounces of Ketchup**
- **4 Ounces of Bourbon**
- **1 Ounce of Honey**
- **1 tsp. of Crushed Red Pepper**

Directions:

1. Slice the pork loin into 6 pork chops.
2. Season the pork with the pepper, salt, and a bit of coconut oil.
3. Wrap it in plastic wrap and place it in the fridge.
4. Peel and pit the peaches. Puree the peaches until they are smooth and pass it through a strainer. Keep the juice.
5. Put the juice in a large pot with the red pepper.
6. Add in the bourbon and allow it to burn off.

7. Add the honey and the ketchup and simmer the mixture for 5 minutes.
8. Remove the pork and lightly mark on the grill. Put it in the pan.
9. Brush the sauce on the pork and roast it at 350 degrees Fahrenheit.
10. Cook the pork until it reaches 145 degrees Fahrenheit internally.

Nutritional Information:

- Calories: 440
- Total Fat: 12g
- Saturated Fat: 8g
- Carbohydrates: 40g
- Protein: 32g

Coconut Butter Beef Brisket

Ingredients:

- 2-3 Pounds of Beef Brisket
- 2 Tbsp. of Onion Soup Mix
- ½ Cup of Coconut Butter
- 1/8 Cup of Dijon Mustard

Directions:

1. Preheat the over to 300 degrees Fahrenheit.
2. Place the brisket in a roasting pan (fat side up).
3. In a medium mixing bowl, combine the soup mix, coconut butter, and mustard.
4. Spread it evenly on top of the meat.
5. Cover the pan with a lid or aluminum foil.
6. Cook the meat for 3-4 hours.

Nutritional Information:

- Calories: 72
- Total Fat: 6g
- Saturated Fat: 3g
- Carbohydrates: 0g
- Protein: 6g

Hawaiian Harvest Pork Chops

Ingredients:

- 1 Tbsp. of Coconut Oil
- 4 Large Pork Center Chops
- 1 Medium Onion – Sliced
- 2 Apples – Cored, Sliced
- 2 Garlic Cloves – Minced
- 2 Tbsp. of Flour
- ½ Cup of Dark Beer
- 1 Cup of Chicken Broth
- 1 tsp. of Cinnamon
- 1 tsp. Of Ginger
- 1 Tbsp. of Thyme
- Salt
- Pepper

Directions:

1. Add the oil to a large skillet.
2. Brown the pork chops on both sides.
3. In the same frying pan, sauté the onions until they are translucent.
4. Add the garlic and the apples.
5. Sprinkle the flour into the pan drippings.
6. Deglaze the pan with the beer.

7. Add the rest of the listed ingredients; cover it and turn it to medium heat for 1 hour.

Nutritional Information:

- Calories: 286
- Total Fat: 13g
- Saturated Fat: 5g
- Carbohydrates: 0g
- Protein: 39g

Cheesy Sausage Hawaiian Pizza

Ingredients:

- ½ Cup of Pineapple
- ½ Cup of Flakes Coconut
- 8 Ounces of Italian Sausage – Cooked, Crumbled
- 1 – 10 Ounce prepared Pizza Crust – Thin
- ½ Cup of Pizza Sauce
- 2 Cups of Provolone Cheese – Shredded
- 1 – 4 Ounce Can Mushrooms Pieces – Drained

Directions:

1. Preheat your oven to 450 degrees Fahrenheit.
2. Spread the pizza crust evenly with the sauce, one cup of cheese, and all other ingredients.
3. Top with one more cup of cheese.
4. Bake the pizza on the oven rack for 10 minutes.

Nutritional Information:

- Calories: 220
- Total Fat: 8g
- Saturated Fat: 4g
- Carbohydrates: 28g
- Protein: 12g

Coconut Marinated Grilled Shrimp

Ingredients:

- 3 Cloves of Garlic – Mined
- 1/3 Cup of Coconut Oil
- ¼ Cup of Tomato Sauce
- 2 Tbsp. of Red Wine Vinegar
- 2 Tbsp. of Basil
- ½ tsp. of Salt
- ¼ tsp. of Cayenne Pepper
- 2 Pounds of Shrimp – Peeled, De-Veined
- Skewers

Directions:

1. In a large mixing bowl, stir together coconut oil, garlic, tomato sauce, and vinegar.
2. Season with salt, basil, and pepper.
3. Add the shrimp to the bowl, and stir it until all the shrimp was covered.
4. Cover the shrimp and refrigerate it for 30 minute to 1 hour.
5. Preheat the grill over medium heat.
6. Thread the shrimp onto the skewers, piercing once near the head, and then through the tail.
7. Lightly oil the grill grate.

8. Cook the shrimp on the grill for 2-3 minutes on each side.

Nutritional Information:

- Calories: 416
- Total Fat: 22g
- Saturated Fat: 12g
- Carbohydrates: 41g
- Protein: 15g

Garlic and Coconut Prime Rib

Ingredients:

- 1 – 10 Pound Prime Rib
- 10 Cloves of Garlic – Minced
- 2 Tbsp. of Coconut Oil
- 2 tsp. of Salt
- 2 tsp. of Black Pepper
- 2 tsp. of Thyme

Directions:

1. Place the prime roast in a roasting pan (fatty side up).
2. In a medium-mixing bowl, add the coconut oil, garlic, salt, thyme, and pepper.
3. Spread the mix over the fatty part of the prime roast and allow it to sit at room temperature for 45 minutes.
4. Preheat your oven to 500 degrees Fahrenheit.
5. Bake the prime roast for 20 minutes, and then reduce the heat to 325 degrees. Continue baking for 60-75 minutes.
6. Allow the prime roast to rest for 10-15 minutes before you cut it.

Nutritional Information:

- Calories: 537
- Total Fat: 24g
- Saturated Fat: 10g
- Carbohydrates: 0g
- Protein: 58g

Firecracker Coconut Grilled Alaska Salmon

Ingredients:

- 8 – 4 Ounce Salmon – Fillet
- ½ Cup of Coconut Oil
- 4 Tbsp. of Soy Sauce
- 4 Tbsp. Of Balsamic Vinegar
- 4 Tbsp. of Green Onions – Chopped
- 3 tsp. of Brown Sugar
- 2 Cloves of Garlic – Minced
- 1 ½ tsp. of Ground Ginger
- 2 tsp. of Red Pepper Flakes
- 1 tsp. of Sesame Oil
- ½ tsp. of Salt

Directions:

1. Place the filets in a medium glass dish.
2. In a medium-mixing bowl, combine the oil, soy sauce, green onions, vinegar, brown sugar, ginger, garlic, pepper, salt, and sesame oil. Whisk it together thoroughly.
3. Pour it over the fish and cover it. Allow it to sit in the refrigerator for 4-6 hours.
4. Prepare the grill with coals 5 inches away from the grate.

5. Grill the fish for 5 inches from the coals for 10 minutes for each inch of thickness.

Nutritional Information:

- Calories: 280
- Total Fat: 13g
- Saturated Fat: 3g
- Carbohydrates: 0g
- Protein: 39g

Pork Chops with Raspberry Coconut Sauce

Ingredients:

- ½ tsp. of Thyme
- ½ tsp. of Sage
- ¼ tsp. of Salt
- ¼ tsp. of Pepper
- 4 – 4 Ounce Boneless Pork Loin Chops
- 1 Tbsp. of Coconut Butter
- 1 Tbsp. of Coconut Oil
- ¼ Cup of Raspberry Jam – Seedless
- 2 Tbsp. of Orange Juice
- 2 Tbsp. of White Wine Vinegar
- 4 Sprigs of Thyme

Directions:

1. Preheat the oven to 200 degrees Fahrenheit.
2. In a small mixing bowl, combine the sage, thyme, salt, and pepper.
3. Rub it evenly onto the pork chops.
4. Melt the coconut butter and coconut oil in a nonstick pan.
5. Cook the pork for 4-5 minutes on each side (turning once).

6. Remove the pork and put it in the preheated oven in a pan to keep it warm.
7. In another skillet, combine the jam, vinegar, and juice. Bring it to a boil and cook it for 2-3 minutes.
8. Spoon the sauce on top of the pork chops.

Nutritional Information:

1. Calories: 218
2. Total Fat: 7g
3. Saturated Fat: 4g
4. Carbohydrates: 0g
5. Protein: 14g

Pineapple Coconut Chicken Tenders

Ingredients:

- ½ Cup of Pineapple Juice
- ½ Cup of Coconut Butter
- 1/3 Cup of Light Soy Sauce
- 2 Pounds of Chicken Breast Strips
- Skewers

Directions:

1. In a small pan on medium heat, add the juice, coconut butter, soy sauce, and brown sugar.
2. Remove it from the heat just before it begins to boil.
3. Put the chicken in a medium bowl. Cover it with the marinade; refrigerate for 30 minutes.
4. Preheat the grill on medium heat.
5. Thread the chicken lengthwise on the skewers.
6. Oil the grill grate lightly. Grill the chicken for 5 minutes on each side.

Nutritional Information:

1. Calories: 144
2. Total Fat: 5g
3. Saturated Fat: 0g
4. Carbohydrates: 15g
5. Protein: 14g

Thank You!

We thank you for your support and welcome you into the recipe junkies family! Reviews are always greatly appreciated.

Check out some of these best sellers on Amazon. All of our books are formatted both in paperback and eBook for your convenience.

Recipe Junkies is growing and we appreciate all of our newsletter subscribers! **You are not just a number to us.** Join our popular newsletter and see all of the awesome offers we have for our subscribers. Like us on Facebook and Twitter as well. Open the **FREE** previews on Amazon and find our clickable links to our newsletter and other offers, or email **recipejunkies1@gmail.com** for more information.

Disclaimer:

All rights reserved. No part of this book may be reproduced or transmitted in any form or by any means, electronic or mechanical, including photocopying, recording or by any information storage and retrieval system, without written permission from the author, except for the inclusion of brief quotations in a review. The information provided in this book is designed to provide helpful information on the subjects discussed. This book is not meant to be used, nor should it be used, to diagnose or treat any medical condition. For diagnosis or treatment of any medical problem, consult your own physician. The publisher and author are not responsible for any specific health or allergy needs that may require medical supervision and are not liable for any damages or negative consequences from any treatment, action, application or preparation, to any person reading or following the information in this book. References are provided for informational purposes only and do not constitute endorsement of any websites or other sources. Readers should be aware that the websites listed in this book may change.

Printed in Great Britain
by Amazon.co.uk, Ltd.,
Marston Gate.